·FRESH FROM THE OVEN·

COOKIES & BISCUITS

KEN FIN

Contents

ALMOND COOKIES

MAKES 10-15

1 cup (4 oz, 125 g) rice flour or ground rice
1/2 cup (3 oz, 90 g) raw sugar
2 cups (8 oz, 250 g) ground almonds
3/4 cup (6 oz, 185 g) unsalted butter
1 tablespoon iced water
30 whole blanched almonds

Sift rice flour into a bowl, stir in sugar and ground almonds. Add butter and work in with your hand, with a squeeze-and-knead action to form a stiff dough. The mixing can be done with a food processor but may have to be finished off by hand. Finally knead and squeeze in the iced water.

Roll tablespoons of mixture in clean, cool hands into balls. Put on greased baking trays 1 inch (2.5 cm) apart, flatten slightly and top each with an almond.

Bake at 350°F (180°C, Gas Mark 4) for 12 minutes or until delicately browned. Cool on wire cooling trays.

Garnish: Arrange wedges of nectarine in a fan shape, peeled lychees on two thirds of individual dessert plates. Place 2 to 3 almond cookies on each plate and serve.

BAKED MARZIPAN

SERVES 12

1 1/2 lb (750 g) very finely ground almonds
3/4 teaspoon almond extract (essence)
3 cups (1 1/2 lb, 750 g) superfine (caster) sugar
3 egg whites, lightly beaten

Gently heat the almonds, almond extract, and sugar together until warm enough to knead into a smooth paste. Blend in the egg whites. Form into desired shapes with the fingers or press into patty tins. Arrange on a greased baking sheet (oven tray) and bake in a preheated oven (300°F, 150°C, Gas Mark 2) until marzipan feels dry.

Tip: The marzipan can be glazed by dipping into sugar syrup and briefly toasted under a hot broiler (grill) to brown the tops.

BRANDY SNAPS

2 oz (60 g) butter or margarine
2 oz (60 g) superfine (caster) sugar
2 oz (60 g) light treacle (golden syrup)
2 oz (60 g) all-purpose (plain) flour
¹/₄ level teaspoon ground ginger
1 cup (8 fl oz, 250 ml) heavy (double) cream
few pieces stem or crystallized ginger, finely chopped

Line three or four baking trays with parchment (baking paper). Grease two or three wooden spoon handles.

Over a gentle heat melt butter in a saucepan with sugar and treacle; take off heat. Sift flour and ginger together and beat into melted mixture. It is essential to bake snaps in batches, putting the mixture onto cold baking trays. Keeping them well spaced, put four teaspoons of mixture onto lined baking trays.

Cook in moderate oven (325°F, 170°C, Gas Mark 3) for about 10 minutes or until an even golden brown. Cool briefly, pushing edges back into shape with a small round-bladed knife, then carefully ease off paper, one at a time. Immediately wind round a greased wooden spoon handle then quickly shape the others before they set. If the mixture becomes too firm, return to oven for a minute or so, then try again.

Cool on a wire rack until firm, then slide off handles. Cook and shape the remaining mixture in the same way. The mixture will keep in an airtight container for up to 2 weeks.

To serve, whip cream until stiff and if desired add a few pieces of ginger. Fill snaps using piping bag fitted with large star piping nozzle.

CHEESE STRAWS

MAKES 30

2 cups (8 oz) self rising (raising) flour
1 teaspoon salt
1/4–1/2 teaspoon cayenne pepper (to taste)
4 oz (125 g) cheddar cheese, finely grated
3 oz (90 g) Copha (white vegetable shortening), melted and cooled
2 tablespoons cold water

Preheat the oven to 230°C (450°F, Gas Mark 8). Lightly grease the baking trays with polyunsaturated oil.

Sift together the flour, salt and cayenne pepper and thoroughly mix in the grated cheese.

Add the water to the melted Copha and pour it over the flour-cheese mixture, mixing to form a firm dough. Roll the dough thinly, then cut it into strips 1/4 inch x 4 inch (6 mm x 10 cm) and twist each strip slightly.

Bake for 10 minutes. Turn onto wire racks to cool.

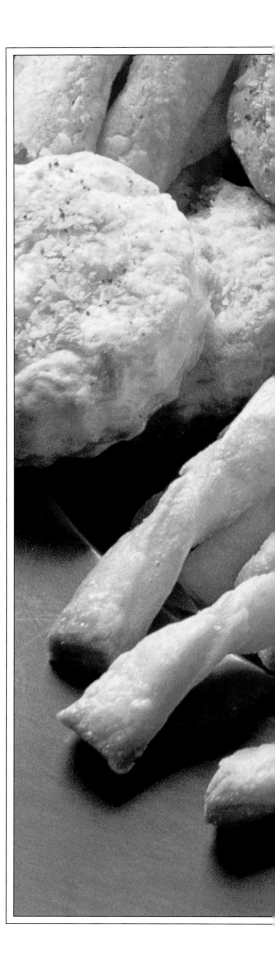

CHOCOLATE PINWHEELS

MAKES 48–60

8 oz (250 g) butter
1 ³/₄ cups (12 oz, 375 g) superfine (caster) sugar
2 eggs
2 teaspoons vanilla extract (essence)
3 ¹/₂ cups (14 oz, 440 g) all-purpose (plain) flour
1 ¹/₂ teaspoons double-acting baking powder (3 teaspoons baking powder)
¹/₂ teaspoon salt
¹/₂ tablespoon cocoa
¹/₂ teaspoon ground cinnamon

Cream butter and sugar in a mixing bowl, add eggs, vanilla and beat well. Sift and add flour, baking powder, and salt. Divide mixture in half. Add cocoa, and cinnamon to half mixture. Shape each half into a rectangle ¹/₄ inch (6 mm) thick. Put one on top of the other, roll up tightly, wrap in waxed (greaseproof) paper, chill, then slice thinly.

Bake in a moderate oven (350–375°F, 180–190°C, Gas Mark 4–5) for 10 to 15 minutes.

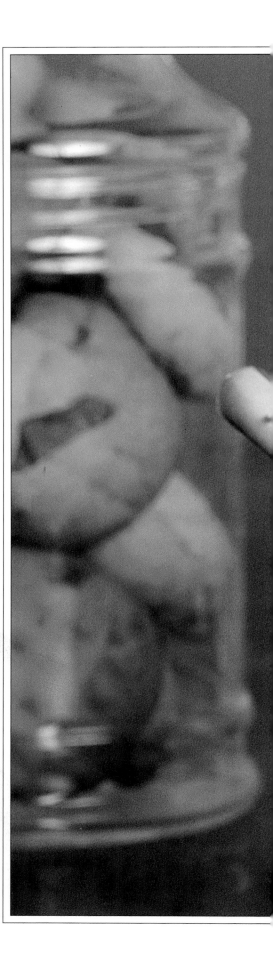

CHOCOLATE WALNUT CREAMS

MAKES 12

4 oz (125 g) butter
³/4 cup (6 oz, 185 g) superfine (caster) sugar
¹/2 teaspoon vanilla extract (essence)
1 ¹/2 cups (6 oz, 185 g) all-purpose (plain) flour
1 tablespoon cocoa
¹/2 teaspoon double-acting baking powder (1 teaspoon baking powder)
pinch of salt
¹/2 cup (2 oz, 60 g) chopped walnuts
¹/4 cup (2 fl oz, 60 ml) milk

CHOCOLATE CREAM ICING:

1 cup (5 oz, 155 g) confectioners' (icing) sugar
2 teaspoons cocoa
1 tablespoon softened butter
1–2 tablespoons condensed milk

Cream butter, sugar, and vanilla until light and fluffy. Sift dry ingredients and blend in with walnuts and milk. Place generous teaspoonfuls in rough mounds on greased baking trays and bake in a moderate oven (350–375°F, 180–190°C, Gas Mark 4–5) for 20 to 25 minutes until cooked. Cool on a wire rack and sandwich cookies together with icing.

Chocolate cream icing: Sift confectioners' sugar and cocoa into a mixing bowl. Add softened butter and blend to a spreading consistency with condensed milk.

COCOA BROWNIES

4 oz (125 g) semi-sweet (plain) chocolate
5 oz (150 g) butter or margarine
12 oz (375 g) superfine (caster) or light soft brown sugar
1/2 teaspoon vanilla extract (essence)
4 eggs
5 oz (150 g) all-purpose (plain) flour, sifted
2 oz (60 g) walnuts or other nuts, finely chopped
3 oz (90 g) seedless raisins
little sifted cocoa powder or about 4 oz (125 g) semi-sweet (plain)
or white chocolate, melted

Line a rectangular pan 11 x 7 x 1 1/2 inches (28 x 18 x 4 cm) with parchment (baking paper).

Break up chocolate and put in an ovenproof bowl with butter. Melt over a pan of gently simmering water, then beat in sugar and vanilla until smooth. Beat in the eggs one at a time until smooth and evenly mixed.

Fold in the flour, then nuts and raisins. Mix until evenly blended, then pour into the pan.

Cook in a moderate oven (350°F, 180°C, Gas Mark 4) for about 50 minutes or until well risen, firm to the touch and just shrinking away from the sides of pan.

Leave to cool in pan then remove carefully and peel off paper. Dredge generously with cocoa powder or spread with the melted chocolate, swirling it around. Leave to set.

To serve, cut into fingers or squares.

COCONUT MACAROONS

MAKES 20-24

2 cups (6 oz, 180 g) unsweetened (desiccated) coconut
1 teaspoon cream of tartar
3 teaspoons cornstarch (cornflour)
4 egg whites, at room temperature
1 ¹/₃ cups (10 oz, 315 g) superfine (caster) sugar
1 teaspoon vanilla extract (essence)

Grease baking trays and dust lightly with cornstarch. Combine coconut, cream of tartar, and cornstarch in a bowl; toss lightly to mix.

Whisk egg whites in a glass bowl until frothy and soft peaks form; gradually add sugar, beating well after each addition.

Add the vanilla then quickly but lightly fold in the coconut mixture — do not overmix.

Drop in rough teaspoonfuls onto trays, put in a pre-heated very cool oven (250°F, 120°C, Gas Mark ¹/₂) and bake for 40 to 45 minutes, until dry and crisp.

Open oven door and cool in oven for 30 minutes; remove and when cold store the macaroons in an airtight container.

COCONUT RASPBERRY DAINTIES

MAKES 40

1 cup (4 oz, 125 g) all-purpose (plain) flour
1/2 scant cup (3 oz, 90 g) superfine (caster) sugar
4 oz (125 g) butter or margarine
1 1/3 cups (4 oz, 125 g) unsweetened (desiccated) coconut
1 egg
3 tablespoons raspberry jelly (jam)

Sift flour into a mixing bowl, add sugar, rub in butter. Stir in coconut and mix to a firm dough with beaten egg. Knead lightly then roll out thinly. Cut into rounds with a 2 inch (5 cm) cutter. Cut the middle out of half the rounds with a 1 inch (2.5 cm) cutter. Place cookies on a greased baking tray, allowing a little room to spread.

Bake in a moderate oven (350–375°F, 180–190°C, Gas Mark 4–5) for 12 to 15 minutes until golden brown. When cool, spread rounds with raspberry jelly and place a ring on top. If desired sprinkle a little extra coconut in the middle of each cookie.

COFFEE KISSES

MAKES 36

2 cups (8 oz, 250 g) self-rising (raising) flour
pinch of salt
4 oz (125 g) butter or margarine
$^1/_2$ scant cup (3 oz, 90 g) superfine (caster) sugar
1 egg
1 teaspoon instant coffee
1 tablespoon hot water

COFFEE CREAM:
1 teaspoon instant coffee
1 tablespoon hot water
1 $^1/_5$ cups (6 oz, 185 g) confectioners' (icing) sugar
2 oz (60 g) butter

Cookies: Sift flour and salt. Cream butter and sugar in a mixing bowl, beat in egg. Dissolve instant coffee in hot water and add to mixture alternately with the flour. Mix thoroughly. Pipe through a forcing bag and plain pipe on to a greased baking tray.

Bake in a moderately slow oven (325–350°F, 160–180°C, Gas Mark 3–4) for 12 to 15 minutes, cool, then sandwich together with coffee cream.

Coffee cream: Dissolve instant coffee in hot water and cool. Sift confectioners' sugar. Soften butter and beat to a cream. Gradually beat in sugar and coffee.

CORNFLAKE CRUNCHES

1 cup butter
³/₄ cup (5 ¹/₂ oz, 170 g) superfine (caster) sugar
1 egg
2 ¹/₂ cups (10 oz, 310 g) all-purpose (plain) flour
1 teaspoon double-acting baking powder (2 tablespoons baking powder)
2 cups (3 oz, 90 g) cornflakes, lightly crushed
2 tablespoons glacé cherries

Cream butter and sugar until light and fluffy. Add the egg and beat well. Sift the flour and baking powder and fold into the mixture. Form mixture into small balls and roll in cornflakes. Place on a greased baking sheet (oven tray) and flatten with a fork. Cut cherries into small pieces and put a piece on top of each cookie.

Bake in a moderate oven (350–375°F, 180–190°C, Gas Mark 4–5) for 10 to 12 minutes. Cool on a wire rack.

CREAM AND JELLY KISSES

MAKES 20

COOKIES:

4 oz (125 g) butter
1 cup (7 oz, 220 g) sugar
1 teaspoon vanilla essence
1 egg
2 ³/4 cups (11 oz, 345 g) flour sifted
1 ¹/2 teaspoons baking powder
¹/4 teaspoon bicarbonate of soda (baking soda)
¹/2 cup (4 fl oz, 125 ml) milk

BUTTER CREAM FILLING:

2 tablespoons softened butter
1 cup (5 oz, 155 g) confectioners' (icing) sugar, sifted
¹/2 teaspoon vanilla essence
2 tablespoons condensed milk

JELLY (JAM) CREAM FILLING:

1 tablespoon jelly (jam) — such as raspberry jelly (jam)
4 tablespoons confectioners' (icing) sugar
2 teaspoons softened butter

Cookies: Cream together the butter and sugar with the vanilla essence. Add the egg, beating the mixture well. Sift together the dry ingredients and add alternatively with the milk, beating well, to make a dough. Cover and chill the dough.

Preheat the oven to 180°C (350°F, Gas Mark 4). Roll the dough out thinly and cut into rounds, or shapes. Bake on a greased sheet for 10 minutes. Turn onto a wire rack to cool, then stick together with butter cream or jam (jelly) filling.

Butter cream filling: Beat together half of the icing sugar and the softened butter. Add the vanilla essence and then the condensed milk. Beat in the remaining icing sugar.

Jelly (jam) cream filling: Combine ingredients together to make a smooth spreadable filling.

CUSTARD CREAMS

MAKES 30

8 oz (250 g) butter
1 cup (7 oz, 220 g) superfine (caster) sugar
1 egg
1 teaspoon vanilla extract (essence)
2 ¹/₄ cups (10 oz, 315 g) all-purpose (plain) flour
¹/₂ cup (3 oz, 90 g) custard powder
³/₄ teaspoon double-acting baking powder (1 ¹/₂ teaspoons baking powder)

BUTTER ICING:

1 cup (5 oz, 155 g) confectioners' (icing) sugar, sifted
2 tablespoons butter, softened
¹/₂ teaspoon vanilla extract (essence)
2 tablespoons condensed milk

Cream butter and sugar until light and fluffy. Gradually beat in egg and vanilla. Sift dry ingredients and fold into mixture. Break off pieces and roll into small balls. Place on ungreased baking trays and press down with a fork. Bake in a moderate oven (350–375°F, 180–190°C, Gas Mark 4–5) for 15 minutes. Cool on a wire rack. When cool, join pairs together with butter icing.

Butter icing: Gradually beat half the confectioners' sugar into the softened butter, add vanilla. Beat in condensed milk and add remaining sugar.

FESTIVE MACAROONS

7 egg whites
2 1/2 cups (1 lb, 500 g) superfine (caster) sugar, sifted
1 lb (500 g) finely ground blanched almonds, sifted
2 tablespoons rose water or orange water

Preheat oven to 250°F (120°C, Gas Mark 1/2). Thoroughly grease baking trays.

Beat egg whites until dry, then gradually add all the sugar. Add rose water to ground almonds, mixing well; gradually blend this into egg white-sugar mixture. Drop spoonfuls onto trays, allowing room to spread.

Bake for 30 minutes; cool on trays.

FLORENTINES

3 oz (90 g) butter
4 oz (125 g) superfine (caster) sugar
4 oz (125 g) flaked almonds
1 oz (30 g) seedless raisins, chopped
1 1/2 oz (40 g) mixed peel, chopped
1 1/2 oz (40 g) glacé cherries, chopped
finely grated peel (rind) of 1/2 lemon or orange
1 oz (30 g) crystallized pineapple or papaya (paw paw), finely chopped
1 oz (30 g) stem or preserved ginger, chopped (optional)
about 6 oz (175 g) semi-sweet (plain) chocolate, melted

Line three baking trays with parchment (baking paper). Melt butter and sugar in a saucepan and boil for 1 minute. Take off heat and stir in remaining ingredients except the chocolate. Leave to cool.

Heap teaspoonfuls of mixture on baking trays, keeping well apart — a maximum of four per sheet for safety.

Cook in moderate oven (350°F, 180°C, Gas Mark 4) for 10 to 12 minutes or until golden brown. As they cool, push the cookies back into shape with a small palette knife. Using the knife, carefully place on a wire rack and leave until quite cold and firm.

Melt chocolate either in a microwave or in a heatproof bowl over a pan of gently simmering water. Spread over back (the smooth side) of each Florentine and as it sets, mark into wavy lines with a fork. Leave to set.

They will keep for a week without the chocolate, between sheets of waxed (greaseproof) paper in an airtight container. Spread with chocolate just before serving.

HEALTHY BAKLAVA

MAKES 20

1 cup (4 oz, 125 g) chopped walnuts
1 cup (4 oz, 125 g) chopped almonds or filberts (hazelnuts)
2 oz (60 g) lecithin meal
2 1/4 tablespoons raw sugar
2 tablespoons toasted wheatgerm
1 teaspoon ground cinnamon
pinch of ground cloves
about 17–18 sheets filo pastry
6 oz (185 g) unsalted butter, melted

HONEY SYRUP:

1 cup (8 fl oz, 250 ml) water
3/4 cup (9 oz, 270 g) honey
1–2 tablespoons lemon juice
piece of cinnamon stick
3 whole cloves

Mix together the walnuts, almonds, lecithin meal, sugar, wheat germ, cinnamon, and cloves.

Lightly butter the base of a shallow baking dish. Line base of dish with a sheet of filo pastry, brush with melted butter and repeat with seven more sheets, brushing each with butter. Spread half the nut mixture over. Cover with two more sheets of pastry, brushing each with butter. Spread the rest of the nut mixture onto the pastry. Place seven or eight more sheets of pastry on top, brushing each with butter, including the top layer.

With a very sharp knife, neatly trim away any pastry overlapping the edges of the dish. Mark diamond patterns in the surface, cutting through the top couple of layers of pastry. Sprinkle with a little cold water (this creates a crispy surface).

Bake on a low shelf in the oven (325°F, 160°C, Gas Mark 3) for 30 minutes, then move up to a higher shelf and bake for 30 minutes more. Remove from oven and cut Baklava into diamond shapes. While still hot, spoon honey syrup over.

Honey syrup: In a saucepan mix together all the ingredients, bring to a boil, then simmer for about 10 minutes. Strain, and pour over the Baklava. Stand for at least 4 hours before serving.

HONEY WAFERS

MAKES 16

4 oz (125 g) butter, softened
6 oz (180 g) superfine (caster) sugar
2 tablespoons honey
3 oz (90 g) all-purpose (plain) flour, sifted
2 egg whites

Cream butter and sugar until light and fluffy. Stir in honey and flour.

In a separate bowl, beat the egg whites until white and frothy, then stir into the mixture.

Line two baking trays with parchment (baking paper) and drop spoonfuls of the mixture onto the trays, leaving room for wafers to spread to about 3 inches (7 $^1/_2$ cm) across. Cook in two batches.

Bake in a moderate oven (350°F, 180°C, Gas Mark 4) for about 15 minutes until golden brown.

Leave on trays for about 1 minute then put on a cake rack to cool.

Keep in an airtight container.

MIXED NUT BARS

4 oz (125 g) butter, softened
2 tablespoons confectioners' (icing) sugar
2 teaspoons vanilla extract (essence)
¹/₂ cup (2 oz, 60 g) cornstarch (cornflour), sifted
¹/₂ cup (2 oz, 60 g) all-purpose (plain) flour
1 oz (30 g) ground almonds
1 oz (30 g) very finely chopped filberts (hazelnuts)
1 oz (30 g) very finely chopped unsalted peanuts
1 oz (30 g) semi-sweet (dark) chocolate

Preheat oven to 350°F (180°C, Gas Mark 4). Grease baking trays.

Beat the butter, sugar, and vanilla together until fluffy and light textured. Sift cornstarch, flour, and ground almonds together, fold into butter-sugar mixture and mix well. Spoon mixture into a piping bag fitted with a ¹/₂ inch (1 cm) serrated nozzle. Pipe "sticks" of mixture 3 inches (8 cm) long onto baking trays allowing room to spread. Carefully top with a light layer of filbert-peanut mixture.

Bake for 15 minutes. Cool on wire racks. Melt chocolate in a double boiler (saucepan) and carefully coat half of each stick; allow to set.

OATMEAL CARROT COOKIES

MAKES 24

6 oz (185 g) butter
³/4 cup (6 oz, 185 g) sugar
1 cup grated raw carrot
1 egg
2 teaspoons lemon rind
1 ¹/4 cups (5 oz, 155 g) all-purpose (plain) flour
¹/2 teaspoon salt
1 teaspoon double-acting baking powder (2 teaspoons baking powder)
1 cup (5 oz) rolled oats

Cream butter, cream in sugar, beat in carrot and egg, and blend well. Mix in lemon rind, flour, salt, and baking powder sifted together. Stir in rolled oats. Place teaspoons of dough onto a buttered baking tray.

Bake in a preheated oven (375°F, 190°C, Gas Mark 5) for 10 to 12 minutes or until cookies are a delicate brown around the edges. Loosen from pan while still warm, cool on a rack, and store in airtight containers. They freeze well.

OLD FASHIONED CHOCOLATE COOKIES

MAKES 30

2 cups (8 oz, 250 g) all-purpose (plain) flour
1/2 teaspoon baking soda (bicarbonate of soda)
pinch of salt
4 oz (125 g) butter
2 oz (60 g) unsweetened (cooking) chocolate
1 cup (5 oz, 155 g) dark brown sugar, firmly packed
1 egg
1 teaspoon vanilla extract (essence)
1/2 cup (4 fl oz, 125 ml) milk

CHOCOLATE GLAZE:

1 oz (30 g) unsweetened (cooking) chocolate
1 tablespoon butter
1 1/2 tablespoons hot water
2 tablespoons cream
1 cup (5 oz, 155 g) confectioners' (icing) sugar
pecan nuts

Sift together flour, baking soda, and salt and set aside. Cut butter into pieces and put in a heavy saucepan. Add chocolate and melt over low heat. Take off heat and stir in sugar. Add egg and vanilla to the warm chocolate mixture and stir until smooth. Stir in half of sifted dry ingredients. Then, very gradually, just a few drops at a time at first, stir in the milk. Add remaining dry ingredients and stir briskly until completely smooth.

Use a dessertspoon of dough for each cookie. Place in even mounds 2 inches (5 cm) apart on greased baking trays. Bake in preheated oven (350°F, 180°C, Gas Mark 4) for 12 to 15 minutes, turning trays around to ensure even baking. The cookies are done when tops spring back firmly if lightly touched with a fingertip.

Let stand for a moment then turn out and cool on a wire rack.

Chocolate glaze: Melt chocolate with the butter in the top of a small double boiler (saucepan) over hot water. Take off heat and stir in hot water and cream. Add confectioners' sugar and stir until smooth. If necessary, add a little more water or sugar to make a consistency like heavy cream sauce. With a small metal spatula, smooth glaze over tops of cookies, keeping about 1/2 inch (1 cm) away from edges. Top each cookie with a pecan nut. Stand for a few hours to dry.

PEANUT BUTTER COOKIES

MAKES 60

4 oz (125 g) butter
$1/2$ cup (3 $1/2$ oz, 100 g) superfine (caster) sugar
$1/2$ cup (4 oz, 125 g) peanut butter
1 egg
1 $1/2$ cups (6 oz, 185 g) all-purpose (plain) flour
$1/4$ teaspoon double-acting baking powder ($1/2$ teaspoon baking powder)
peanut halves to decorate
milk to glaze

Cream butter, sugar, and peanut butter in a mixing bowl. Add beaten egg and mix well. Sift flour and baking powder and mix into butter mixture to form a firm dough. Roll out on a floured board until $1/4$ inch (5 mm) thick. Cut into rounds with a small fluted biscuit cutter and place on greased baking sheets (oven trays). Lightly press a peanut half into the middle of each biscuit. Glaze with milk.

Bake in a moderately hot oven (375–400°F, 190–200°C, Gas Mark 5–6) for 12 to 15 minutes. Lift off with a spatula and cool on a wire rack.

PISTACHIO TREATS

MAKES 16

2 egg whites
4 oz (125 g) superfine (caster) sugar
1 1/2 oz (40 g) all-purpose (plain) flour, sifted
1 3/4 oz (45 g) butter, melted and cooled
few drops almond extract (essence) (optional)

TO DECORATE:

2 oz (60 g) semi-sweet (plain) chocolate, melted
1 1/2 oz (40 g) pistachio nuts, blanched and finely chopped

Line two baking trays with parchment (baking paper). Grease two or three thick skewers or narrow pencils.

Whisk egg whites in a grease-free bowl until very stiff and dry and standing in peaks. Gradually fold in sugar, then flour and finally melted butter and extract until evenly but lightly mixed.

Spread mixture fairly thinly into oblongs about 4 x 3 inches (10 x 7.5 cm), placing only two or three per baking sheet.

Cook in a fairly hot oven (400°F, 200°C, Gas Mark 6) for about 8 minutes or until lightly browned.

Remove cookies one at a time, using a round-bladed palette knife and place upside down on another piece of parchment. Quickly roll around skewers or pencils. Slide off quickly and cool on wire rack. If cookies become too firm to roll, return briefly to oven to re-soften.

To decorate: Melt chocolate and dip one or both ends of the cookies in chocolate so they are evenly coated and then sprinkle with chopped pistachio nuts. Leave to set.

ROLLED COOKIES

MAKES 36

2 cups sugar
2 cups shortening (lard)
1 egg, lightly beaten
1 teaspoon grated nutmeg
¹/4 teaspoon salt
2 cups (16 fl oz, 500 ml) buttermilk
1 teaspoon baking soda (bicarbonate of soda)
enough flour for rolling dough

Preheat the oven to 350°F (180°C, Gas Mark 4). Grease the baking sheets (oven trays).

Cream the sugar and shortening together. Beat in the egg, nutmeg, and salt.

Combine the buttermilk with the baking soda, and add this to the mixture. Add sufficient flour to make the mixture into a rollable dough. Roll out to ¹/4 inch (5 mm) thick, and cut into shapes.

Bake for 10 to 12 minutes. Allow to cool on wire racks.

SAVORY SWIRLS

³/₄ cup (3 ¹/₂ oz, 100 g) large, black olives, pitted (stoned)
1 teaspoon capers
2 anchovy filets
¹/₄ cup (2 oz, 60 g) sun-dried tomatoes
¹/₄ cup (2 fl oz, 60 ml) olive oil

BISCUIT (SCONE) DOUGH:

1 ¹/₂ cups (6 oz, 180 g) self-rising (raising) flour
2 oz (60 g) butter
1 cup (8 fl oz, 250 ml) buttermilk or milk
2 tablespoons (1 ¹/₂ fl oz, 45 ml) buttermilk, to glaze
1 egg yolk, to glaze

Put olives, capers, anchovies, and tomatoes in a blender or food processor. Blend until smooth. With the motor running, add oil in a thin steady stream, allowing mixture to thicken as it blends.

Biscuit dough: Sift flour into a bowl. With your fingertips, rub butter into the flour. Add buttermilk and mix to form a manageable dough. Lightly knead the dough on a floured board until smooth. Roll out dough to form a rectangle ³/₄ inch (1 ¹/₂ cm) thick. Spread mixture over dough, leaving a 1 inch (2 cm) border then roll up starting from one of the longer sides.

Cut into 1 inch (2 cm) slices. Place the swirls very close together on a greased baking tray. Mix buttermilk and egg yolk together and brush over tops. Bake in a fairly hot oven (425°F, 220°C, Gas Mark 7) for 15 to 20 minutes or until golden and cooked through.

SWEDISH CHRISTMAS COOKIES

MAKES 36

2 yolks from hard-cooked (boiled) eggs
3 oz (90 g) butter
$1/3$ cup (3 oz, 90 g) superfine (caster) sugar
$1/3$ cup (3 fl oz, 90 ml) thick sour cream
zest from $1/2$ lemon
zest from $1/2$ orange
1 raw egg yolk
1 cup (4 oz, 125 g) all-purpose (plain) flour, sifted
$1/8$ teaspoon baking soda (bicarbonate of soda)
$1/8$ teaspoon salt
1 egg white, well beaten
1 tablespoon superfine (caster) sugar
1 tablespoon ground almonds

Preheat oven to 325°F (160°C, Gas Mark 3). Grease baking trays.

Mash egg yolks with butter to make a smooth paste. Blend in sugar, mixing well. Add sour cream, lemon, orange zest, and egg yolk.

Sift together flour, baking soda, and salt; add to other ingredients, mixing well, adding more flour if necessary to make a firm, rollable dough. Roll out to $1/4$ inch (5 mm) thick and cut into fancy shapes, such as stars or animals, brush with beaten egg white, and sprinkle with sugar-almond mixture.

Bake for 15 to 20 minutes. Turn onto wire racks to cool.

WALNUT MERINGUE SQUARES

MAKES 30

4 oz (125 g) butter
³/₄ cup firmly packed brown sugar
1 teaspoon vanilla essence
2 egg yolks
1 ¹/₂ cups plain flour
1 teaspoon baking powder
1—2 tablespoons milk

MERINGUE TOPPING

2 egg whites
pinch salt
³/₄ cup firmly packed brown sugar
¹/₂ teaspoon vanilla essence
¹/₂ cup chopped walnuts

Beat butter, sugar and vanilla essence until light, add egg yolks and beat well. Sift dry ingredients and mix into creamed mixture with milk. Spread in a greased 12 x 10 inch (30 x 25 cm) Swiss Roll tin.

Bake in a moderately hot oven for 10 minutes. Spread with meringue topping and return to oven to cook for further 25 to 30 minutes. Cool in tin and cut into 2 inch (5 cm) squares when cold. Lift out with a spatula.

Meringue Topping: Beat the egg whites with salt until stiff and gradually add brown sugar, beating well until stiff, glossy peaks form. Fold in the vanilla essence and walnuts.

GEM BISCUITS (SCONES)

MAKES 24-36

2 oz (60 g) butter
4 oz (125 g) superfine (caster) sugar
2 eggs
1 1/2 cups (6 oz, 185 g) self-rising (raising) flour
pinch salt
3/4 cup (6 fl oz, 180 ml) milk

While oven is preheating (425°F, 200°C, Gas Mark 7), put in ungreased gem irons to heat.

Cream butter and sugar together, gradually add beaten eggs, beating well between each addition. Sift flour and salt together and add alternately with the milk, folding gently until batter is an even consistency.

Remove heated gem irons from oven, brush them with butter and half fill with batter. Bake in oven for 10 to 15 minutes. Turn onto a wire rack and when cold split and spread with butter.

PLAIN BISCUITS (SCONES)

MAKES 12–14

2 cups (8 oz, 250 g) self-rising (raising) flour
¹/₂ teaspoon salt
1 oz (30 g) butter or margarine
³/₄ cup (6 fl oz, 180 ml) milk

Sift flour and salt into a mixing bowl. Rub butter into flour with fingertips until the mixture resembles fine breadcrumbs. Using a round-bladed knife, quickly mix in milk to make a soft dough. Turn dough onto a lightly floured board, sprinkle top of dough with flour and knead lightly until smooth. Roll out to ³/₄ inch (2 cm) thick and cut into rounds with a floured cutter.

Place biscuits onto a greased baking sheet (oven tray). Glaze with a little milk and bake in a very hot oven (450–500°F, 230–250°C, Gas Mark 8–9) for 12 to 15 minutes. Place biscuits (scones) on a wire rack. When cool break in halves and spread with butter or serve with strawberry jelly (jam) and whipped cream.

Golden raisin (sultana) biscuits: Before adding the milk add ¹/₂ cup (3 oz, 90 g) golden raisins and 1 tablespoon superfine (caster) sugar.

Cheese biscuits: Before adding the milk add ¹/₂ cup (2 oz, 60 g) grated cheese.

Wholewheat (wholemeal) biscuits: Substitute 1 cup (2 ¹/₂ oz, 75 g) wholewheat (wholemeal) self-raising flour for 1 cup (4 oz, 125 g) self-raising flour.

Note: The biscuit dough may also be shaped into a circle, marked into 6 or 8 wedges and baked in a very hot oven for 20 to 30 minutes.

Cooking tip: Instead of rubbing butter into flour, heat butter with 1 teaspoon water until frothy and pour onto flour with milk. The result is just as good.

PUMPKIN BISCUITS (SCONES)

MAKES 20

2 oz (60 g) butter or margarine
2 scant tablespoons superfine (caster) sugar
$^1/_2$ cup cooked mashed pumpkin
1 egg
$^1/_2$ cup (4 fl oz, 125 ml) milk
2 $^1/_2$ cups (10 oz, 315 g) self-rising (raising) flour, sifted

Cream butter and sugar. Add pumpkin and mix well. Add egg and mix in milk a little at a time. Add flour and mix to a soft dough. Turn onto a floured board and knead lightly. Roll out to $^3/_4$ inch (3 cm) thick and cut into rounds with a floured cutter. Place rounds on a greased baking tray.

Glaze with milk and bake in a hot oven (425°F, 220°C, Gas Mark 7) for 15 to 20 minutes. Turn onto a wire rack and when cool break open and spread with butter.

WHOLEWHEAT (WHOLEMEAL) MARMALADE BISCUITS (SCONES)

MAKES 20

1 ¹/₂ cups (6 oz, 185 g) self-rising (raising) flour
1 ¹/₂ cups (1 ¹/₂ oz, 230 g) wholewheat (wholemeal) self-rising (raising) flour
¹/₂ teaspoon salt
2 oz (60 g) butter
1 egg
¹/₂ cup (4 oz, 125 g) marmalade
¹/₄ cup (2 fl oz, 60 ml) milk
extra milk for glazing

Sift flours and salt together twice. Cut butter into mixture with a round-bladed knife then rub in with fingertips. Beat egg and combine with marmalade, then add milk. Combine with dry ingredients and mix to a soft dough with the knife.

Knead lightly on a floured board and roll out to ³/₄ inch (2 cm) thickness. Cut into rounds with a floured biscuit (scone) cutter. Place biscuits (scones) on a greased baking sheet (oven tray). Brush tops with milk to glaze.

Bake in a hot oven (400–450°F, 200–230°C, Gas Mark 6–8) for approximately 15 to 20 minutes or until golden brown.

Serve warm with butter.

This edition published in 1996 for KEN FIN
An imprint of Social Club Books Pty Ltd
6–10 Keele Street, Collingwood Victoria 3066, Australia
Ph: (03) 417 6699 Fax: (03) 417 5574

© Copyright: Harbour Books 1996
© Copyright design: Harbour Books 1996
Printed in Singapore by Tien Wah Press (Pte) Ltd
ISBN 1 86302 506 5